UNITED STATES
HISTORY IN RHYME

A CHILD'S FIRST HISTORY BOOK:
A MUST READ FOR ALL AMERICANS

LARRY MARKUS

A fun, complete, inspiring, review of U.S. history

WestBow Press books may be ordered through booksellers or by contacting:

WestBow Press
A Division of Thomas Nelson & Zondervan
1663 Liberty Drive
Bloomington, IN 47403
www.westbowpress.com
1 (866) 928-1240

ISBN: 978-1-9736-3677-9 (sc)
ISBN: 978-1-9736-3678-6 (e)

Library of Congress Control Number: 2018909764

Print information available on the last page.

WestBow Press rev. date: 11/21/2018

WESTBOW
PRESS®
A DIVISION OF THOMAS NELSON
& ZONDERVAN

Dedication

I dedicate this book to my wonderful grandchildren:

> Naomi,
>> Beau,
>>> Cort,
>>>> Ellison,

and all the children of the U.S.

All of whom need and must truly learn
> to love their country.

The best way to do that is:
> to know the history of their country
>> and how it has changed
>>> and is changing.

These changes have altered the world
> and its governments.

My hope and dream is:
> that my book will help all children
>> enjoy and love to
>>> read about their country

and develop a burning desire to
> find answers to the questions
>> that this book will bring to their minds.

Epigraph

It is absolutely necessary that we know and remember
our history, or we are bound to repeat it!

About the Book

In 1803, President Jefferson said to James Monroe,
To France you must go:
To try and help our country grow.

To purchase New Orleans is what he would try,
But the whole Louisiana Territory he was able to buy.

This is only a sample of what you will enjoy as you read, *U.S. History in Rhyme*. This book takes the highlights of our history and presents them in a way that will catch a child's attention and adult's, also. It will peak their interest in our history by raising the who and what questions that motivate them to want to know more. For example: Who is Paul Revere? and What was "The shot heard 'round the world?"

In 1492
Columbus sailed the ocean blue.

It's just a little rhyme but it conveys a lot of information and most of all-we remember it! This book contains facts from our history in rhyme that can easily be remembered.

We know that you and your children will love this book and want to read it multiple times.

Preface

When the opportunity presented itself, I conveyed to our new music teacher that it was my desire to have my history classes learn several historical songs about our country and other well-known patriotic songs. I planned to have my students present these songs in concert to the school.

In planning the concert, I decided that each song should have an introduction to place it in its appropriate historical setting. As I began to write the introductions, I realized that it would be fun and entertaining to write them in rhyme and the rest is history.

As I prepped my students for the concert, I determined that this easily could be a play if we had actors dressed for the period presenting their lines. I continued to work on the lines until I had covered the discovery of America until current history. After having the play published, I thought that the rhyming narrative with a few key quotations might sell as a book that would interest all citizens and be an excellent introduction and/or review to history for children and a good resource for learning their history facts.

I truly hope you enjoy this short read of our history and choose to read it more than once. Also, remember to share it with others.

Thanks

Acknowledgements

I want to thank my wife, Vicki, for knocking holes when I hit a wall. I won't mention how many times this happened, but this work would not be complete without her help.

I also want to thank Sharon Counce, Kristy Kelly and Jason Scott, my fellow fifth grade teachers who helped so much to make each play a success. Next, there are my assistants, JoAnn Rochelle and Gwyn Franklin, without whose work I could never have gotten the play to the stage.

Then, of course, there are the music teachers, Sara Thigpen, Doyle and Heather Freeman, who were willing to teach the songs and prepare the students for the presentation. Without their hard work the play would not have been complete.

When the whole play was finished and divided into two parts the fourth-grade teachers, Kathy Burns and Maria Bedsworth, willingly took on the task of preparing their students to present the first part of the play for which fourth grade is academically responsible.

Also, I would like to thank Dr. Nancy Crews who encouraged me to have the play published and who pointed me in the right direction in finding a publisher.

Last of all, I must thank Mary Ann Clayton, our principal, who took the chance that I could present anything worthy of allowing the whole school time out from classes to provide an audience for all our hard work.

I am much obliged to all these people.

Discovery

In 1492,
Columbus sailed the ocean blue.

Like the Vikings, he crossed the Atlantic,
But not to raid,
He was looking for treasures,
For which to trade.

Columbus landing in America

"Westward to Asia!" he told the King he would go.
About America he did not know.
Reports of his trips set the world aglow.

As men explored this new world,
Searching for gold to be more specific,
Balboa traveled across Panama,
And discovered the Pacific.

Magellan found a way around America in 1519:
Then sailed on westward with a crew that became very lean.
Starting with 260 men, they finished with only 18.

After three long years of westward travel,
He proved to all,
That off the earth man would not fall!

Now on such trips, men knew their ships would not leak,
So, for the next 100 years,
for land and treasure they continued to seek.

In 1607, Englishmen came to Jamestown,
And there a colony they did found.

When it looked like this colony would be a wreck,
The growing of tobacco saved their neck.

In 1620, the Pilgrims said to the King,
"If to America you let us go,
In our chosen religion we can grow."

Pilgrim Fathers Leaving England

With the King's religion many others disagreed.
They also realized America would fill their need.

People came to America searching for a faith,
On which they could lean,
Until the number of colonies became thirteen.

Map of original thirteen colonies

Revolution

In 1765, the King stabbed the colonists in the backs, (pockets that is)
And all the colonies he began to tax.

The Boston Tea Party aroused the nation.
They began to shout,
"No Taxation Without Representation." (1773)

The Boston Tea Party

Still the King heeded not their plea,
So, the Patriots began to sing,
"Revolutionary Tea."

Listen my children and you shall hear,
Of the midnight ride of Paul Revere.
On this famous ride,
He called the minutemen to his side. (4/18/1775)

Paul Revere Ready to Ride

The next day the British intended to stop
This Revolutionary whirl,
But someone fired, "The shot heard around the world."

"The shot heard around the world"

Patrick Henry gave the Patriots their rallying cry,
When he said he would rather die.
In his speech before the Virginia House of Burgesses
on Mar. 23, 1775,

Patrick Henry

"If this be treason,
Make the most of it,
Is life so dear, or peace so sweet,
As to be purchased at the price of chains and slavery?
Forbid it, Almighty God!
I know not what course others may take, BUT AS FOR ME,
GIVE ME LIBERTY OR GIVE ME DEATH!"

On July 4th, 1776,
"The Declaration of Independence"
Thomas Jefferson wrote,
Then they sent the King
This inflammatory note.

Signing the Declaration of Independence

"We hold these truths
To be self-evident,
That all men are created equal,
That they are endowed by their Creator
With certain unalienable Rights,
That among these are
Life, Liberty and the Pursuit of Happiness."

In Philadelphia,
The Liberty Bell did ring
And the Patriot soldiers
Did march and sing.

Their favorite song was "Yankee Doodle."

Liberty Bell

Betsy Ross in her duty did not lag:
She got busy and sewed our first battle flag.

Now the Patriot army found its pride,
And behind George Washington
they did ride.

George Washington Crossing the Delaware River

Our great cause, to France,
Benjamin Franklin so well laid,
That the French agreed to come to our aid.

Benjamin Franklin

British Surrender at Yorktown, VA

After fighting for 7 long years
And the shedding of many fears and tears,
In 1781, after the victory at Yorktown,
Peace and liberty were finally found.

Government

In-order-to get freedom right,
The Constitution they begin to write. (1778)

James Madison was the man
With a governing plan.
For his government intuition,
He is called "The Father of the Constitution."

James Madison
"Father of the Constitution"

James Madison stated, "Liberty may be
endangered by the abuse of liberty
But also by the abuse of power."

Founding Fathers at the Constitutional Convention

Preamble to the Constitution

"We the People of the United States,
In-order-to form a more perfect Union,
Establish Justice, Insure Domestic Tranquility,
Provide for the Common Defense,
Promote the General Welfare,
And secure the blessings of Liberty to ourselves and our Posterity,
Do ordain and establish this Constitution
for the United States of America."

For the first President, George Washington they did elect,
And because of all his great leadership,
"Father of Our Country" is the epitaph they did select. (1789)

President George Washington

"I hold the maxim no less applicable to public than to private
affairs, that honesty is the best policy." -George Washington

Still the people could not see all of freedom's lights,
So, they got busy and added the Bill of Rights. (1791)
For which-sadly-we must continue to fight!

Bill of Rights

The Bill of Rights

1. Freedom of religion, speech and press.
2. Right to bear arms.
3. Freedom from quartering soldiers.
4. Freedom from illegal searches.
5. Right to due process of law.
6. Right to a speedy and public trial.
7. Right to a trial by jury of peers.
8. Freedom from cruel punishment.
9. Other rights of the people.
10. Powers granted to the states.

Expansion I

Land to the mighty Mississippi,
England did cede,
And the restless Americans were looking for people to lead.

On the western frontier our country began to grow,
And men like Daniel Boone, to Kentucky,
Was a-raring to go.

Dan'l Boone heading westward to Kentucky

But Dan'l was not the only favorite son,
In Tennessee there was Andy Jackson
And in Lawrence County Tennessee,
Davy Crockett was the one.

David Crockett

In 1803, President Jefferson said to James Monroe,
To France you must go:
To try and help our country grow.

To purchase New Orleans is what he would try,
But the whole Louisiana Territory he was able to buy.

The French again came to our aid,
At four cents an acre, fifteen million dollars,
Is all we paid.

Louisiana Purchase

With the Louisiana Purchase,
The size of our country did double,
But taking it from the Indians,
Would be a lot more trouble.

Throughout our history, we did the Indians many wrongs,
Because of this the poets wrote many songs,

In retaliation the Indians took many people's hair,
The end of the Indian wars we will now share.

In 1877 Chief Joseph of the Nez Perz said,
"I am tired of fighting.
I want to look for my children.
Maybe I shall not find all of them among the dead.
Hear me my chiefs!
I am tired!
My heart is sick and sad!
From where the sun now stands,
I will fight no more, forever."

Chief Joseph, "I will fight no more, forever."

As our great nation expanded,
President Jefferson an exploration commanded. (1804-1806)

Lewis and Clark were commissioned to explore;
To search, to inquire, to map, and more.

Lewis and Clark

Only to the mountains,
Was written in our new deed,
But over the mountains and to the ocean,
Lewis and Clark their expedition did lead.

Three years later, they did return,
And told the people all they did learn.

They reported that in Oregon everything so much better did grow,
So, to Oregon the restless Americans wanted to go.

A road developed over prairies, hill and dale.
It became known as the Oregon Trail.

War of 1812

In 1812, England and the U.S.
Were back at war.
And until this day,
We still wonder what for.

During this war, America's future
Was influenced by two great battles.

At New Orleans, Andrew Jackson,
Led America to victory.
For his great exploits,
He became known as Ol' Hickory. (1814)

On this popularity,
To the presidency,
He did ride.
And gave the common people
Their first presidential pride. (1829-1837)

Andrew Jackson defending New Orleans.

At Fort McHenry,
While the cannons did rattle,
Francis Scott Key,
In a victorious manner,
Put pen to paper and wrote,
The "Star Spangled Banner,"

Our nation was wowed,
By the words he allowed.
Now everyone sings them,
As our National Anthem.

Fort McHenry

Expansion II

Down in Northern Mexico the land was bare,
Mexico invited Americans to settle there. (1820's)

"Gone to Texas"
The words on the empty houses said,
As hope for a better life many people were led.

As Texas became populated by U.S. citizens,
To Mexico's laws, they did not wish to listen.

Santa Anna would not leave them alone,
At the Alamo, they rebelled and became a country all their own. (1836)
To again be U.S. citizens,
Their hearts did yearn.
Can Texas become a state?
They decided to learn.
To Congress
They made their request.
In 1845, Texas became a state,
Like all the rest.

The Alamo

When Texas became a state,
The Mexican government cried aloud,
America's peaceful skies began to cloud.

Soon with Mexico a war did begin, (1846-1848)
When it was over,
The U.S. had grown again.
California and the four corners area,
Were now part of our kin.

In 1849, along The Oregon Trail, many
Americans to California were bound.
At Sutter's Mill, "in them thar" mountains,
Gold had been found!
All the rowdy miners turned California
Into such a shape.
The people there decided they wanted to become a state. (1850)

California Gold Miners

As the wagon trains moved slowly west,
They were carrying some of America's best.
To enjoy a better life, their musical instruments they brought along.
And at night, around the campfires, they would all sing along.

49er's Singing Around the Nightly Campfire

Civil War

Slavery was allowed when our country did begin.
And then rapidly expanded,
With the invention of Eli Whitney's cotton gin. (1794)

Slaves Picking Cotton

As the idea of slavery began to be deplored,
Ways to free them began to be explored.

Many slaves felt that death,
Was the only hope of freedom that was left.
In hopes of hastening this event,
They would often sing these laments.

Their favorites were:
"Swing Low, Sweet Chariot"
And
"Go Down Moses"

The development of the Underground Railroad,
Was the route to freedom that many slaves rode.

Famous underground railroad conductor Harriet Tubman
Had this to say,
I didn't come into this world a slave to stay.
And wasn't going to stay ONE.
Her dash to freedom
SHE BRAVELY WON.
Thirteen times to the south she went back
And helped other slaves, their bag to pack.
As they followed the "Drinking Gourd"
their hands and feet became sore.
But with them their trials and dangers she bore,
And the number of free people became even more. (1850-1863)

Harriet Tubman Helping Slaves Escape.

The opposing views about slavery became such a force,
Eleven states of our country tried to get a divorce. (1860-1861)

From the planting of these rebellious seed,
To the Civil War these activities did lead.

In 1860, following Robert E. Lee,
and his rebel band,
The Confederates marched off to war singing "Dixieland."
A good military leader, the Yankees, at first could not find,
But the soldiers seemed not to mind.
They bravely marched to battle singing this line.
"The Battle Hymn of the Republic."

Civil War Battle

When President Abraham Lincoln
Issued the Emancipation Proclamation,
The United States became a slave free nation.

President Abraham Lincoln with Emancipation Proclamation in hand

In 1863 Abe said,
"Now therefore, I, Abraham Lincoln, President of the United States,
By the virtue of the power in me vested,
As Commander-in-chief,
Do order and declare,
That all slaves, are and henceforward, shall be free."

Freed Slaves Searching for New Homes.

Then Abe said, "Not much longer can this country bleed."
He called U.S. Grant the northern army to lead.

As Grant's army pushed southward
The rebel lines began to bend.
In April of '65, at Appomattox, Virginia
He brought the awful war to an end.
With the South in total destruction,
The country now turned to Reconstruction.
(1867-1877)

General Lee Surrendering to General Grant

Transportation

No story about America would be complete,
Without discussing the ways men found
To avoid Traveling on their Feet.

First, they moved about on river boats,
Then they built canals so that large cargos they could float.

Early Canal Boats

Early on they traveled over land on crude woodland trails,

Traveling Long Distances by Horseback Was Slow, Tiring and Dangerous

With the advent of the steam engine they took to the rails.

Early American Train

Building railroads all across the land,
Allowed this country to rapidly expand.
Till finally, in 1869, at Utah's Promontory Point,
The country was joined from "sea to shining sea,"
When they drove the golden spike joint.

The steam engine also spawned the Industrial Revolution,
To millions of poor Americans this was their financial solution.

Then Henry Ford gave them the car, (1913)
Now, all Americans could afford to travel afar.
With all this new travel
Our woodland trails began to unravel.
To handle all these heavy loads,
America began to build better roads.
As man's love for the car became such a relation,
The U.S. became an interstate connected nation. (1956)

Early American Car

From the beginning of time man has wanted to fly,
In 1903, at Kitty Hawk in North Carolina,
The Wright Brothers gave it one more try.

One of the Wright Brothers' First Planes

After their successful flight,
Business men saw another transportation light.
As air travel continued to grow,
To space, man next wanted to go.
Russia, smeared egg in our face,
When they were first to put a man into space. (1961)
In 1961 President John F. Kennedy
Challenged Americans to
commit America to achieving this goal,

"Before this decade is out,
We will land a man on the moon
and return him safely to Earth."

By this Americans were inspired
And we remember what transpired.
In the space race, we caught up rather soon,
In 1969, an American was first to walk on the moon.

Astronaut Neil Armstrong stepping onto the Moon's
surface on July 20, 1969 said: "That's one small step
for (a) man but one giant leap for mankind."

Communication

Moving mail on foot and stagecoach was not the best,
So, America's postal service established the Pony Express. (1860)

Vintage Telegraph

With the invention of the telegraph and Morse's code, (1844)
On wires, messages now swiftly rode.

Still our communication system was not doing so well,
So, the telephone was invented by Alexander Graham Bell. (1876)

Alexander Graham Bell Using Early Telephone

Then the radio and T.V. found their place in the American home,
But now all over the world on the Internet we roam.

Radio invented in 1895
TV invented in 1927

Immigration

In the 1800's, East of the Atlantic, too many people were being born,
And the land there was very worn.
Word spread throughout the eastern continents three.
About the home of the brave and the land of the free.

People there by the "Go to America" bug were bitten.
They longed to see the Statue of Liberty (1886)
And hear the words there written.

Statue of Liberty

"The New Colossus" by Emma Lazarus

"Not like the brazen giant of Greek fame,
With conquering limbs astride from land to land;
Here at our sea-washed, sunset gates shall stand.
A mighty woman with a torch,
Whose flame is the imprisoned lightning.
And her name
Mother of Exiles.
From her beacon-hand
GLOWS WORLD-WIDE WELCOME;
Her mild eyes command
The air-bridged harbor
That twin cities frame.
'KEEP ANCIENT LANDS YOUR STORIED POMP!'
Cries she with silent lips.
'Give me your tired,
Your poor,
Your huddled masses yearning to
BREATH FREE,
The wretched refuse of you teeming shore.
Send these,
The homeless, tempest-tossed to me.
I lift up my LAMP
Beside the GOLDEN DOOR.'"

America grew to be a great nation,
By the routes of immigration.

"America is God's Crucible,
The great Melting Pot
Where all the races of Europe
Are melting and reforming!...
GOD IS MAKING THE AMERICAN."
By
Israel Zangwell

Immigrants Landing at Ellis Island, NY

Expansion III

Problems in Cuba and sinking of the Maine,
Led the U.S. to a war with Spain. (1898)
The "Rough Riders" taking of San Juan Hill,
Turned out to be Teddy Roosevelt's presidential bill. (1901-1909)

In the Spanish-American war the U.S. took control.
Now the world knew America's power was on a roll.
From this war the U.S. grew some more,
And spread its borders beyond its mainland shores.

The Indians had always loved and lived on the mountains and plains.
But now the railroads were bringing more people on trains.
Homestead farmers were praying for more rains.
While the cowboys began riding the range.

Cowboy Riding the Range

With writers making up amazing stories for monetary gains,
Everyone fell in love with the mountains and plains.
So to maintain some scenic places for wild animals and larks,
President Theodore Roosevelt started our system of National Parks.

"Old Faithful" in Yellowstone National Park

1900 To 1950

In the early 1900's in Europe,
Germany wanted more land,
So, its borders it began to expand.

World War I was about to begin,
America was in it before it did end. (1914-1918)

Our doughboys put up a great fight,
When they were finished the world enjoyed the peaceful light.

American World War I Soldiers
"Doughboys"

After the war, America began to progress,
The Roaring Twenties were the signs of success.

Roaring Twenties Dancers

People's prosperity did not last long,
In 1930, the Great Depression came along,

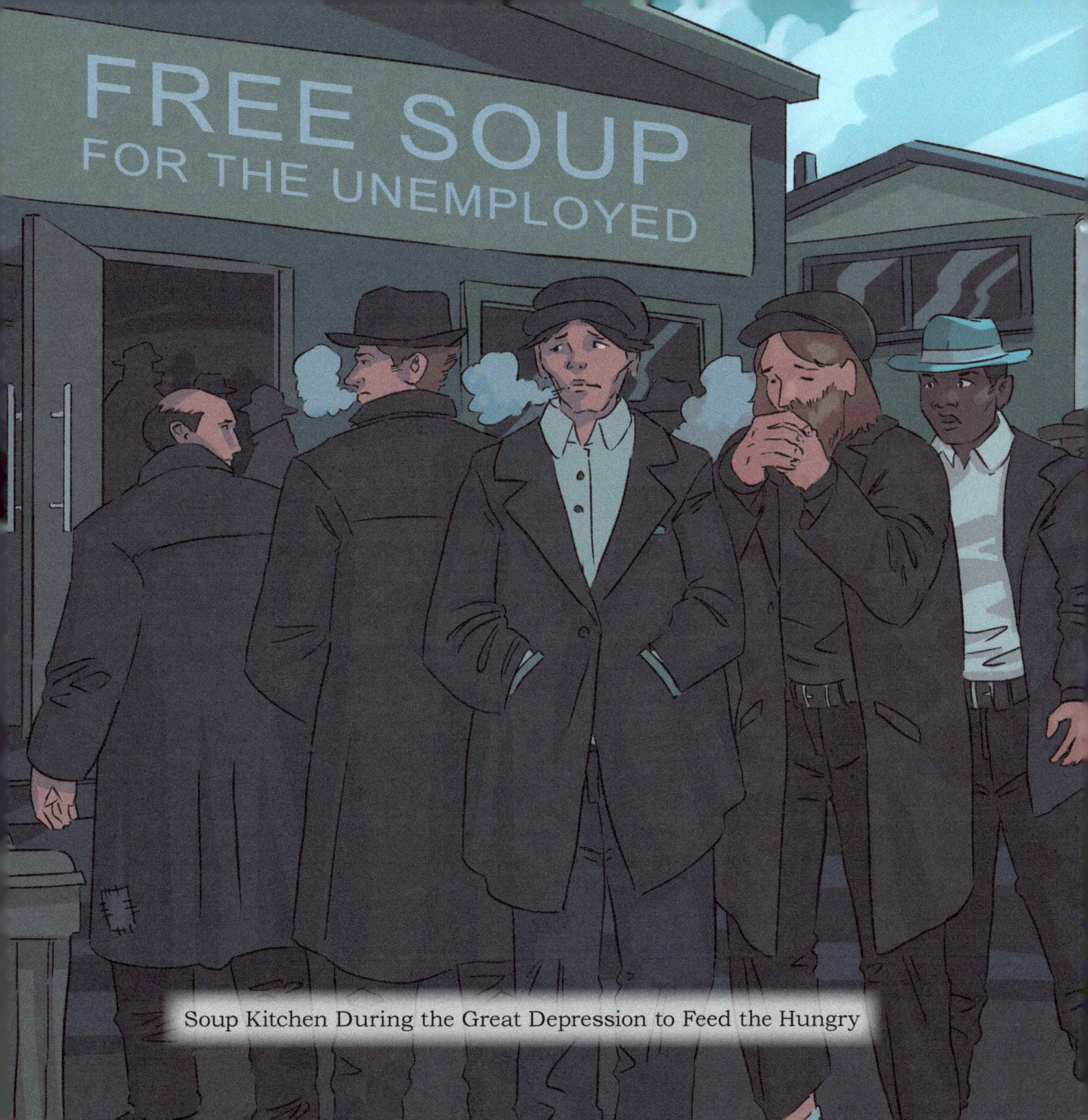

Soup Kitchen During the Great Depression to Feed the Hungry

To describe man's dealing with all the hard times,
There was no shortage of musical lines.

Franklin D. Roosevelt's "New Deal"
Provided many people another meal. (1930's)

As the Great Depression was coming to an end,
World War II was about to begin. (1939-1945)
Hitler's German Army was on the move as before,
But America was not interested in war any more.

When Pearl Harbor was attacked by Japan, (1941)
America's part in this awful war began.

Fighting this war was not any fun,
But when it was over America and its Allies had won.

U.S World War II Soldiers in Battle

The world now wanted to live in peaceful relations,
So, they all got together and created the "United Nations." (1945)

1950's Through 2010

America's desire and willingness to see freedom spread,
To the Korean Conflict our soldiers were led. (1950-1953)

When Communism decided that it wanted to expand,
The Cold War began as America decided
To lend threatened countries a helping hand.

When Communists decided to take South Vietnam,
America went there to build a communist dam. (1955-1975)

This little war grew hotter than Americans desired
Because it wasn't being fought in our own backyard.

This war's guerrilla tactics put American soldiers to the test,
So, the Special Forces were trained to make America's soldiers the best.

The '80's and '90's brought America prosperity and peace.
But on world security the U.S. did not yet have a leash.

In 1990, Iraq's army overran Kuwait,
America's forces didn't have long to wait.
Desert Storm plans were soon laid,
As U.S. forces quickly came to Kuwait's aid.

Korean War Memorial

Helicopter to the rescue in Viet Nam

Special Forces

Silhouette of soldier saluting U.S. Flag

In 2001, terrorist hit America with force.
Now our soldiers were off on a totally new course.
As our army went searching for Osama Bin Laden
Back home our poets were not noddin'.

They stirred up the people with songs and rhymes.
And America began to sing their popular chimes.

My favorites were,
"God bless the USA," by Lee Greenwood

"Where Were You When the World Stopped Turning," Alan Jackson.

"Have You Forgotten," by Darryl Worley

In the presidential race, of 2008,
Martin Luther King Jr's dream sure looked great.

Barack Obama's presidential race wasn't even tight,
As an African-American, moved into the world's spot light.

Terrorists Attack Twin Towers in New York City, New York

When he began the future did not look so bright.
He promised to lead America right.
His leading words shone an old and true light,
When he spoke in his opening address,
"Let us mark this day with remembrance,
of who we are and how far we have traveled.

On this day, we gather because we have chosen hope over fear,
Unity of purpose over conflict and discord.

In reaffirming the greatness of our nation,
We understand that greatness is never a given.
It must be earned with
Hard work and honesty,
Courage and fair play,
Tolerance and curiosity,
Loyalty and patriotism.
These things are old.
These things are true.
They have been the quiet force of progress throughout our history.
What is demanded then is a return to these truths.

What is required of us now is a new era of responsibility,
A recognition,
On the part of every American,
That we have duties to ourselves, our nation, and the world,
Duties that we do not grudgingly accept
But rather seize gladly..."

President Barack Obama Delivering His Inauguration Speech

The Fights for Equal Rights

In the Constitution,
Written by men,
Equal rights, the women,
Did not win.

John Adams' wife, Abigail, made the first call.
She requested they make equal citizens of all.

Her request was in for a fall
As women were left holding the ball.

While some were trying to set the slaves free,
Women asked all, their plight also to see.
At the women's convention at Seneca Falls,
they launched the fights
To win women their voting rights.
When Cady Stanton said in 1848,

Women's Suffrage Movement

"The history of mankind is a history of repeated injuries
And usurpations on the part of man toward woman,
having in direct object the establishment of an absolute tyranny over her.
To prove this, let facts be submitted to a candid world.
HE has never permitted her to exercise her inalienable right to VOTE...
He has made her, if married, in the eye of the law, civilly dead.
He has taken from her all rights in property,
even to the wages she earns...
He has denied her the facilities for obtaining a thorough education,
All colleges being closed against her."

African-American Sojourner Truth said:
"We'll have our rights; just you wait and see if we don't!
Look at me! I have plowed and planted,
and gathered crops into barns,
and no man could outdo me!
AND AIN'T "I" A WOMAN!!"

Sojourner Truth
Illustrated by Kelly Cooper Markus

For the next 70 years, their placards they continued to tote.
Finally, in 1920, women were given the vote.

To win the "War of Wars"
American's men and women, black and white,
Had worked and fought shoulder to shoulder,
But in the 1950's many began to realize
That the fight for, EQUALITY FOR ALL, was not over.

Depictions of Rosie the Riveter;
women's first symbol of female power in industry.

In the work place women knew they were not getting a fair deal,
When they went to pay their bill(s).
They began asking for equal pay
For equal work they did each day.
They also began demanding proper respect,
From "men" whose proper behavior they did neglect.

Martin Luther King Jr. tried, peacefully, to win
African Americans their Civil Rights.
They continued pressing for a fair deal
Until 1964 when President Johnson
Signed the Civil Rights Bill.
African Americans could finally
move beyond the past.
They now had hopes of being free at last.

The American Creed

The making of this Great Nation
Bound together people of odd relations.
These relations developed a unique breed
That called for a special creed:

The American Creed

I believe in the United States of America as a government of the people,
By the people, for the people;
Whose just powers are derived from the consent of the governed;
A democracy in a republic; a sovereign nation of many sovereign states;
A perfect union, one and inseparable;
Established upon those principles of freedom, equality, justice,
and humanity for which American patriots
sacrificed their lives and fortunes.
I therefore believe it is my duty to my country to love it,
To support its constitution, to obey its laws,
To respect its flag, and to defend it against all enemies.

Written by William T. Page
(Accepted by the House of Representatives
On April 3, 1918)

Thank you for reading America's book,
Lay it aside and later take another look.
Share it rather than laying it on a nook.
God bless you and
God bless the UNITED STATES of AMERICA!!!

Epilogue

As I bring an end to this book
At some inspiring words we'll take a look.
In order to be great citizens
To our great leaders we must listen.

The founder and leader of Boston's Sons of Liberty,
Samuel Adams, had as his life-long watchword,
"Equal liberty for myself and ALL my fellow citizens."

To reinforce that we remember JFK's Admonition,
"My fellow Americans,
Ask not what your country can do for you,
but rather ask what YOU can do for your COUNTRY."

With these thoughts in mind I say,
One thing of ALL citizens we must depend:
Against ALL enemies, both foreign and DOMESTIC,
The Constitution We Must DEFEND!

Because Ben Franklin said,
"If we don't all hang together,
We most assuredly will All hang separately."

So still today, if we all hang together,
It will always be as F.D.R. said,
"The only thing we have to fear is,
FEAR Itself."

Before they go vigorously pushing their agendas,
Individuals, special interest groups and political parties
Need to heed Davy Crockett's rule,
"I have this rule for others when I'm dead,
Be always sure you're right-then go ahead."
Knowing that George Washington still expects of us today
His charge to the Constitutional Convention,
"Let us raise a standard to which the wise and honest can repair;
The rest is in the hands of God."

Concerning the 'Freedom of the Press,'
We must NEVER forget Thomas Jefferson's admonition,
"I had rather have a watchdog and no government,
Than have a government and NO watchdog."

My words of wisdom do not belong in this section,
But I want to share them anyway.
I always told my students,
You can't study too much
Because there's no such thing as getting TOO SMART.
And my ball players were told,
You can't practice too much
For there's no such thing as getting TOO GOOD.

Finally, my motto for life and my class was:
The BEST WAY to do anything is the RIGHT WAY.
And
The RIGHT WAY to do EVERYTHING,
Is the BEST WAY.

We want to end this book with a forward look,
Remembering Ben Franklin's desire,
"God grant that not only the love of liberty but a thorough
knowledge of the rights of man may pervade all the
nations of the earth, so that a philosopher may set his foot
anywhere on its surface and say: 'This is my country.'"

Much obliged and God Bless

Glossary

Alamo
an old Spanish mission used as a fort,
when attacked by Santa Anna's army of Mexicans
they killed all the Texans.

Bill of Rights
the first ten amendments added to the constitution
that makes this country a free institution.
Example: freedom of the press, religion, and speech.

Canal
a large man-made ditch,
which, when filled with H_2O
barges can go.

Civil Rights
the basic rights
(freedoms)
that should be enjoyed by all citizens
without any fights.

Civil War
when people or sections of a nation
feel they suffer things not right
and it leads to an extraordinary fight.

Common People
the uneducated people of that day
who usually worked for low pay.

Communism
A form of government where
the government owns everything
and controls you,
even the wages earned
and the job you do.

Confederates
the eleven states that in 1860
decided to rebel,
but in 1865 they fell.

Cotton Gin
a machine used to remove seed quickly from cotton.
Now, from cotton,
a lot more money could be gotten.

Crucible
a pot in which a mixture of materials (Ex. Rocks) are melted
to separate them into their pure forms.
People of similar backgrounds
together like to trot.
When you put several in a pot,
they begin to accept each other's cultures a lot.

Democracy
a form of government
where every citizen needs to answer the call,
to vote,
because elections are open to all.

Doughboy
In WWI,
the suits given to U.S. soldiers was to blame
for doughboys being their nickname.

Eastern Continents Three
In Europe, Asia and Africa many people went into motion
to travel westward across the Atlantic Ocean

Emancipation
African Americans would no longer slaves be;
emancipation set them free.

Endowed
Being in possession of something of great worth
such as power or large portions of this earth.

Epitaph
Words about a person on a tombstone
put there after they are gone.

Exile
People who are driven from their homeland
and are left to roam
as they look for a new home.

Expansion
the action of a nation and/or people
into new land going
causing that nation to be growing.

Exploits
chances (risks) that people take
that end up being something great.

Four Corners
the spot in the western United States
where four states come together,
and people there gather
to put their feet on two lines
and stand in four states at one time.
These states are Utah, Arizona, Colorado and New Mexico.

Declaration of Independence
the written document that said
the Thirteen Colonies were rebelling against the English government.
Loyal to the British they would no longer be.
In the future they would be free.

Depression
a time when business activities take a downturn;
jobs and money are hard to earn.

(The) Go to America bug
America put such a tug
on people's hearts
that from their homeland
they decided to depart.

Guerrilla
a soldier who quickly fights and runs away
in order to live and fight another day.

Inalienable rights
are the freedoms we enjoy every day
that cannot be given up or taken away.
Example: life, liberty and the pursuit of happiness.

(The) Industrial Revolution
was the giant leap of business revolution.
For factories it was the mass production solution.

Lament
songs and poems about people dealing
with their sad feeling(s).

Lark
in this book we used the lark
to represent all the birds in the park.

Liberty
Another word for free
which all people want to be.

Louisiana Territory and Purchase
all the land
stretching in a band
from Texas to Canada
and from the Rocky Mountains
to the Mississippi fountains.
The United States purchased all this land
from France, in 1803,
at the price of 15 million dollars
(a very low price).

Melting Pot
see crucible.

Minutemen
before 1776 all male citizens of the 13 colonies
were trained to fight.
They went about their normal lives during the light
but were always ready to fight
at a minute's notice, even at night.

Morse's Code
a system of electrical impulses creating dashes and dots;
these were then transcribed into messages a lot.

New Deal
an F.D.R bill
designed to allow people to earn another meal;
it helped to get money flowing
as back to work more people were going.

Oregon Trail
the wagon road that developed across the prairie, hill, and dale
became known as the Oregon Trail.

Prairie
in the western U.S. the vast grasslands are rolling
between the Rocky Mountains and where
the mighty Mississippi is flowing.

Patriot
people who to the rebellion of the thirteen colonies were true
and whatever was necessary for its success they would do.

(The) Pony Express
was a system for moving mail quickly across the western U.S.
Men on their fast horses rode
as they carried their light mail load.

Posterity
our decedents,
whose freedom
upon us is dependent.

Rebel
one who believes his country is denying him his rights
and against it he decides to fight.

Reconstruction
with the end of the North and South's warring relations
it was time to rebuild the nation.

Republic
a system of government where representatives we elect,
they then meet together to decide which laws and policies to select.

Revolution
when a group doesn't like the government that is in control
that government they try to overthrow.

Roaring Twenties
lots of people lived wild and lively in the 1920's
and spent many more pennies.

Rough Riders
the cavalry soldiers
that Teddy Roosevelt to the Spanish-American War brought
and on San Juan Hill in Cuba they fought.

(The) Shot Heard Round the World
The first shot fired at Lexington Bridge that
started the Revolutionary War.
It ended in operating our government in a new way
and has been changing the way the world is governed until this day.

Slavery
a situation where people own other people
and keep them under their control.
They crush their soul.

Sovereign
a situation
where a government entity has independent authority,
has the right to govern its own institution,
and has its own constitution.

Statue of Liberty
a large statue on Liberty Island
in New York Harbor
of a woman
that gives hope of freedom to all human(s).

Steam Engine
a powerful engine operated by steam.
It was used to run large machines, factories and sew many a seam.

Telegraph
the machine that sent and received Morse's code.
On wires messages swiftly rode.

Underground Railroad
a system of traveling
operated by people willing to break the law
and risk all.
They would help escaping slaves hide by day
and then assist them on their way.
They would hide and sleep during the light
then travel in the darkness of night.

Union
the organization of states
that make up these United States.

United Nations
an organization of the world's nations
created to enhance better world relations
and help solve global situations.

Wagon Train
traveling together in a long line of wagons
which mules and oxen were drag'n.
The places they were go'n
were Oregon
and Californ-[ia].

World War I
a war between 1914 and 1918,
fought in Europe mostly.
To a large part of the world
in money and lives it was costly.

World War II
the huge war fought from 1939 to 1945,
involving a larger part of the world.
It set Europe, Asia and the Pacific Islands in a whirl.

Yearn
When someone wants some-thing
so much
it irritates
like a sting.

Lightning Source UK Ltd.
Milton Keynes UK
UKHW051237081119
353142UK00005B/91/P